Pro

The Essentials

Project Governance

The Essentials

ROD BEECHAM

IT Governance Publishing

Every possible effort has been made to ensure that the information contained in this book is accurate at the time of going to press, and the publisher and the author cannot accept responsibility for any errors or omissions, however caused. No responsibility for loss or damage occasioned to any person acting, or refraining from action, as a result of the material in this publication can be accepted by the publisher or the author.

Apart from any fair dealing for the purposes of research or private study, or criticism or review, as permitted under the Copyright, Designs and Patents Act 1988, this publication may only be reproduced, stored or transmitted, in any form, or by any means, with the prior permission in writing of the publisher or, in the case of reprographic reproduction, in accordance with the terms of licences issued by the Copyright Licensing Agency. Enquiries concerning reproduction outside those terms should be sent to the publisher at the following address:

IT Governance Publishing
IT Governance Limited
Unit 3, Clive Court
Bartholomew's Walk
Cambridgeshire Business Park
Ely
Cambridgeshire
CB7 4EH
United Kingdom

www.itgovernance.co.uk

First published in the United Kingdom in 2011 by IT Governance Publishing.

ISBN 978-1-84928-180-5

FOREWORD

The term 'project' seems to be one whose hour has come – most things seem to be projects these days. There is perhaps an element of fashion in the development of the word – the buzzword which gets the heads of the cognoscenti nodding – but it is also true that there are just more projects about now. The cycle of innovation and change is continually picking up speed. A system that might have run pretty much consistently for a decade or so before will now undergo significant changes on a yearly basis, as new technology offers better solutions. Traditionally, project management has always been an exciting area to work in because it involves guessing at the future and, as history never tires of showing us, we are not very good at it. Even if the mechanics of a project can be broken down into small, familiar steps, there will always be something out there which has not been anticipated and which has the capacity to delay or derail a plan, leading to cost overruns or even abandonment.

To address this problem, the existing literature is awash with worthy methodologies that seek to quantify risks, codify variables and then provide guidance through the process leading towards a glorious and successful conclusion. There is, of course, a place for these texts – they will never become favourites for bedtime reading – but this brief tome by Rod Beecham is almost an antidote to the genre. Focusing on the governance aspects of projects, it provides a rapid and entertaining overview of the area that is so often badly handled by those who should know better. Following its strictures will not guarantee you success – nothing can ever do that – but it will increase your chances of it, providing you are not enticed away from the path which Rod encourages you to follow.

Tim Thornton

General Manager, Campus Operations
The University of Melbourne

PREFACE

There are many excellent books on project governance and project management, but most tend to assume that an organization is capable of implementing the structures and procedures they recommend. In my experience this is rarely the case. In this little book I have tried to focus on practical steps that any organization can take to improve the performance of its projects.

ABOUT THE AUTHOR

Rod Beecham was educated at Monash and Oxford and has delivered 22 projects across the private, public and not-for-profit sectors over the past 15 years. His projects have ranged from small-team overhauls of particular information systems over periods of weeks to large-scale strategic infrastructure projects of 12 months' duration involving global stakeholders. He has published academic papers, reviewed for academic journals, and published more than 60 essays, interviews and reviews on a wide variety of topics in various newspapers and magazines since 1987. He is currently a freelance consultant.

CONTENTS

INTRODUCTION

The great cover-up

Take a moment to reflect on the larger projects undertaken by your organization over the past five years. Why were these projects undertaken? What benefits were envisaged as stemming from them? How is your organization placed now, compared with five years ago? To what extent have these projects contributed to this change (assuming there has been a change)?

Were you able to identify a project that has, without question, made a positive difference to your bottom-line? Perhaps. But I think, if you reflect carefully, you will agree that many of your projects involved a lot of activity for suboptimal results.

We don't hear much about such things. Many analysts and commentators have tried to probe project failures over the years, but they invariably encounter a wall of silence. No one likes to admit failure, and no company will readily admit to blowing hundreds of thousands or millions of investment dollars.

There are good reasons for this, of course. When large sums of money are involved, admission of failure will inevitably attract blame, and blame can translate into expensive legal proceedings and adverse publicity. These, in turn, can have very serious effects on sales and, for listed companies, their share price.

The consequences of silence, however, are probably more expensive in the long run. I know of a company that, when Enterprise Resource Planning (ERP) installations were all the rage, decided to buy SAP and engaged a consulting firm to help them with the installation. One million dollars later, the project was abandoned.

I know also of a very senior executive at another company who purchased some complex and expensive software for his division while overseas, only to discover that it was utterly incompatible with his existing systems. The result was that the company created an entirely new division to justify the purchase of the software.

A third company I know of decided it needed project management expertise and set up a Project Management Office (PMO). However, the PMO was subordinated to the all-powerful Operations division, with the result that the value of its specialist expertise was lost.

Each of these cases illustrates a failure of project governance.

The first indicates inadequate business and systems analyses prior to project initiation, as well as too much responsibility being handed to the external consulting company.

The second indicates the dangers of an undue emphasis being placed on hierarchical status within the organization. The senior executive was, no doubt, competent in many areas, but unilateral decision-making of such a risky kind is generally inadvisable, and that he was supported and protected by his colleagues suggests a disordered set of organizational priorities.

The third case indicates a fundamental misunderstanding of what projects actually are and how they function in an organizational context.

I'm sure you can think of several additional examples of project failures from your own experience.

So, why do projects keep failing?

Partly for the reasons I gave earlier – a combination of misplaced pride and well-grounded fear – but also, I think, because organizations outside the engineering and construction industries have rarely seen a well-managed project and do not, therefore, possess a conceptual template for good project management practice.

This book is for senior executives in those 'non-project' industries who, nonetheless, have to initiate projects and want them to succeed. It is not a beginner's guide to project management: it is a guide to project governance.

What is project governance?

> Project governance is the establishment of organizational understandings and conditions under which projects may be planned and delivered successfully.

There are many ways in which these understandings and conditions might be created, but the important thing is to realize that they are all essentially qualitative. You do not establish project governance by hiring Project Managers, or – as we have seen – by calling on outside help, or even by establishing a PMO. Project governance is the responsibility of top management – of the CEO and his or her executive team.

It is the top layer of the organization that needs to understand what makes projects work and what makes them fail.

Paying for projects

It all starts and ends, like everything else in organizational life, with management accounting.

Just as the steadily increasing number of project failures generates more and more books and courses on project management and more and more project management 'methodologies', so too does it generate more and more complex ways of accounting for projects. Considered as capital-budgeting decisions, projects can be measured in terms of their net present value, discounted cash flow, discounted payback period, accounting rate of return, internal rate of return, and present value index. Indeed, some financial analysts get quite intoxicated with project benefit measurement, taking us beyond mere accountancy to differential calculus, linear programming, statistical theory (regression analysis) and microeconomics. Oh, and I almost forgot earned-value analysis (EVA).

This is all, quite frankly, insane. The financial return on a project is rarely calculable. The key question to answer about a project brings together motivation and means.

The first question to ask when contemplating a project is: how much are we prepared to spend to make it happen?

All else follows.

The investment cost of projects

Once you have decided how much you are prepared to spend, it might seem logical to approach a Project Manager and tell him or her to develop a plan based on the sum you have arrived at. If you do, however, I believe you are setting yourself up for failure.

We have all seen the projects that began with a rigorous process of planning based on a certain sum, were approved, started up, and then proceeded to incur additional, unforeseen costs. Many of them reach completion even though they end up costing twice or three times as much as they were supposed to. This is explicable in terms of the psychology of commitment. The most common capital-budgeting measure is point of no return.

Planning a project will, itself, cost money. People in your organization – not just the Project Manager – will need to give time to it. External advice may be required, which will need to be paid for, and you won't know whether the project is even feasible until the planning is complete.

Project planning is a sunk cost and should be included in the annual operating budget of every one of your business units.

Cost control

When your Project Manager comes back with a detailed project specification indicating how much she or he estimates the project will cost, you should approve the project only if the estimated cost plus 25% is still equal to or less than the amount you are prepared to spend to make it happen.

This is not because Project Managers are incompetent at budgeting; it is because projects, by nature, involve the unforeseen, and the unforeseen invariably adds cost.

Other factors, all connected with poor project governance, also add cost. We shall encounter some of them in the following chapters.

CHAPTER 1: WHY?

A famous ancient building is the Great Pyramid of Giza. It is believed to have taken between 14 and 20 years to construct, concluding around 2650 BC.

A famous modern building is the Sydney Opera House. Much smaller than the Great Pyramid, and constructed with the use of powerful machinery unavailable to Pharaoh Khufu, it took 14 years to complete.

This should give us pause. The Pharaoh, it would appear, was not constrained by costs or labour problems, but the erection, from approximately 5.5 million tons of limestone, 8,000 tons of granite (imported from Aswan) and 500,000 tons of mortar, using only manual labour, of a geometrically precise structure that was originally 146.5 metres high is a phenomenal achievement, however many years it took.

The story of the Sydney Opera House is rather different. A design competition launched in 1955 resulted in victory for the Danish architect, Jørn Utzon, whose inspired idea was the scalloped concept we see in the completed building. However, the original cost of the Opera House was grossly underestimated to ensure public approval for the project. Construction was begun before drafting was complete because the government wanted to show the electors that something was happening and Utzon's interior designs were scrapped to allow for more seating. By the time the Opera House was opened in 1973, it had cost 16 times more than the original estimate.

The difference between the construction of the Great Pyramid and the construction of the Sydney Opera House is that, in the former case, the project was directed by one person with a clear vision of what was wanted, while in the latter case, numerous persons, all with competing and conflicting agendas, confused the project.

It is a fundamental truth of project governance that projects will come in on time and on budget if they are managed by a competent individual reporting to a Steering Committee armed with full powers. They will invariably not come in on time and on budget if the notional Project Manager is constrained by ad hoc committees, advisory boards and numbers of operational stakeholders with competing agendas functioning outside the formal governance structure.

Now, of course, in many types of organization powerful hierarchical structures exist that cannot be bypassed. But they do not have to be bypassed. They can be accommodated in the planning stage, i.e. before the work of executing the project begins.

The need for this is indicated in the table overleaf, which shows what usually happens – as opposed to what is supposed to happen – during the project planning and execution phases.

Purpose	Common attributes of this stage
To do what is to be done.	• A lot of meetings • A lot of Microsoft® PowerPoint® presentations • Considerable revision of the original idea • A lot of anxiety about cost • Pressure for more resources from specialist staff • Frustration and disgust from upper management at specialist staff incompetence.

Clearly, this is dysfunctional.

So why is dysfunction common?

To answer that, I must emphasize the importance of planning.

The importance of planning

It is natural to assume that, if a project fails, it has been mismanaged. This assumption needs to be clarified, however. If you are not a Project Manager, you will assume that mismanagement occurs once things have started happening – i.e. as the limestone is being brought up from the quarry, or as the foundations are being laid at Bennelong Point.

This natural view is actually mistaken. Project mismanagement usually begins well before the execution stage. Project mismanagement occurs in the planning stage.

The most significant problems with projects are traceable to decisions taken – or not taken – *before any visible work has commenced.*

Plan the project, not the outcome of the project

A project is a delivery mechanism. It is a way of taking your organization, or some part of your organization, from its current state to a preferred state. In their eagerness to reach the destination, organizations can neglect the means of transport.

The Apollo 11 space mission, for example, put men on the moon and was a brilliantly conducted project, but NASA had learned the hard way. The tragedy of Apollo 1, when three astronauts were burned to death on the launch-pad, was attributable to sub-standard wiring and plumbing, inadequate understanding of the chemical reaction of Velcro in a 100% oxygen environment, and static discharge from nylon flight suits in contact with nylon flight seats.

North American Aviation, the company that built the doomed command module, had proposed an oxygen/nitrogen mixture for the craft's atmosphere, but NASA had decided against it, partly on the grounds that the omission of nitrogen saved weight. The effect of a pure oxygen design in the case of fire was not considered.

This is an extreme example – mercifully, few project failures result in human death – but it is a way of illustrating the biggest single problem besetting corporate projects: the pressure to 'get on with it' versus the necessity to cross every 't' and dot every 'i' before 'getting on with it.'

This is a particularly common problem with IT-based projects. Contemporary organizations are permeated at every level with information technology. Changing any part of that technology, or implementing new technology, will have far-reaching effects on the organization as a whole, including indirect effects that can be uncovered only through patient investigation and analysis.

As a senior manager you do not want – quite rightly – to be bothered with such details. Nor do you need to be specifically aware of them. But it is very important that you understand that this is why projects can seem to take a long time before getting anywhere, and that the longer and the more exhaustive the analysis and planning, the more likely that the project will result in a successful outcome with no significant time or cost overruns.

Planning doesn't take time, it saves time.

Planning does cost money. But failed projects cost vastly greater amounts of money!

CHAPTER 2: A PROJECT PRIMER

It may seem unnecessary to discuss the basics of projects, but you would be surprised to know how elusive an understanding of them can be. Accordingly, I offer the following 'primer' in the hope that it will help you to embed an understanding of projects across your organization.

There are many definitions for the term project. I prefer the following:

> A project is a temporary endeavour undertaken to create a unique product or service.

The words 'temporary' and 'unique' are the important ones.

Projects are temporary

Projects are temporary because, unlike operational activities, they finish and do not start again.

For example, your organization, like any organization, will have bills to pay. But your accounts payable process does not conclude when you have paid an account; there will always – unfortunately! – be more accounts to pay. This is why accounts payable is an operational activity.

The installation of an accounts payable system, on the other hand, is a project. Like Aristotle's famous description of plot, it has a beginning, a middle and an end. When the system is installed and operational, the project is over.

The outputs of projects are unique

The outputs of projects are unique because, unlike operational activities, they do not recur.

Your accounts payable staff, for example, will follow a process to pay an account, and then will follow the same process to pay another account, and so on. In each case, the output is the same: a paid account.

The output of an accounts payable system project, on the other hand, is the accounts payable system itself, which is unique. (Your organization may have many different information systems, but only one of them will be an accounts payable system.)

The easiest way to think of the difference between projects and operations is to think of the building in which you work. You probably don't work in the Great Pyramid of Giza, or even in the Sydney Opera House; your building is probably less interesting and probably took much less time and a lot less money to complete.

The construction of your building, though – whatever sort of building it is – was a project: a unique object was planned, costed, built and commissioned. It doesn't need to be built again (if it did, you wouldn't be working in it!). But what you do inside that building will be largely operational, whether it's dealing with customers and suppliers, generating monthly reports, managing your sales force, or whatever.

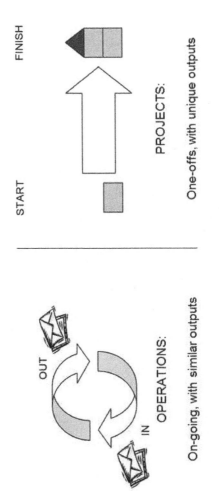

Figure 3: Operations and projects

Why plan a project?

A dangerous confusion exists in many minds between having an idea for a project and actually planning it. **Countless expensive and embarrassing project failures are attributable to this confusion.**

Suppose, for example, you are unhappy with your current accounting system and believe that software package X offers the functions and features you want. It will give you better financial reports, it will speed up the payments process, it will reduce the likelihood of errors and it will be easier for your staff to use. So, in your mind, the plan is to replace your existing accounts payable system with software package X.

But that is *not* the project plan. It is the project's *purpose*.

In a sense, many of the problems that arise from projects can be traced to the use of language. Simple words, such as 'plan', 'goal', 'risk' and 'quality' have very specific meanings in project management that they do not necessarily possess in other contexts. If your organization is to be successful in its projects, it must become familiar with these key project management terms. They are not difficult, but they are crucial.

What is a project plan?

A project plan – which, to avoid confusion, I prefer to call a project specification – is the contract between the project manager and the project stakeholders. It specifies why the project is being undertaken, what it will deliver, when it will deliver it, by whom it will be delivered, and how much it will cost.

Everything in a project plan or specification is quantifiable. A project specification will not say, 'The project will deliver a new accounts payable system.' It will say, 'The project will install software package X in three phases, commencing on [*date A*], [*date B*] and [*date C*] respectively, to deliver [*list of business benefits*], with parallel processing in place until [*date D*], when the old accounts payable system will be decommissioned, at a total cost of [$].' This, specific to the point of pedantry, is the goal of the project.

This book is not a beginner's guide to project management, so I will not talk at length about the various distinctions between key terms, It is, however, very important that the specific meanings of them be understood. Here's a list of the major ones:

Project management term	Meaning
Cost	The total cost of the project to the organization. The project specification will show how the total cost has been arrived at by itemizing the individual costs under categories such as procurement (externally purchased goods and services) and human resources (including the salaries of internal staff allocated to the project, whether on a full- or part-time basis, and on-costs). It will also indicate the source(s) of project funds and how they will be disbursed.
Goal	What the output(s) of the project will be, expressed in terms of precise date(s), precise business benefits(s) and exact cost(s).
Integration	How the project will fit into the larger organizational context, expressed in terms of relative priorities, resource allocation, risk management and conflict resolution.
Issue	An unforeseen problem that arises once the project is underway. Issues are inevitable, but they are much less damaging if the project specification has detailed how they will be prioritized and dealt with as they arise, and by whom.
Plan	The contract between the project manager and the project stakeholders. It will specify the purpose and goal(s) of the project, its scope, its time line, the people and the equipment required, the project organization, reporting and communication principles, the project's quality system, the risks associated with the project and how they will be mitigated, and the criteria to be met for the project to be deemed complete.

Quality	This term does not refer to the quality of the project's output(s) – that is specified in the project goal. Project quality refers to the delivery mechanism itself – the project. Project quality is specified in terms of relevant standards and how to satisfy them (quality planning), regular evaluation of project performance in the form of audits and scheduled tollgates (quality assurance), and monitoring of specific project results to ensure that they comply with the standards set and, if not, to identify and eliminate the causes of unsatisfactory performance (quality control).
Risk	Anything that could or will threaten attainment of the project goal. Risks can be found everywhere: in external dependencies, organizational factors, planning activities, the business case, the technical environment, and so on. The identification of risks and of ways of dealing with them is a critical aspect of the project planning process. The difference between a risk and an issue is that a risk is foreseen.
Scope	This term is not a verb – one does not 'scope' a project. In project management, scope is a noun only, indicating what activities are included in the project and what activities are not included in the project. The scope of the project will be set out precisely in the project specification to eliminate any possibility of jurisdictional friction.

Figure 4: Project management terms

The Steering Committee

The Project Manager drafts the project specification. It will be a large document and will take time to prepare. When the Project Manager is satisfied that the specification is complete, it should be examined by your organization's Internal Auditor or Risk Manager, who will determine whether the costings, schedule and risk assessment are sufficiently robust. If they are, the project specification will then be presented to the Project Steering Committee for approval.

The Steering Committee is the key instrument of project governance.

The relationship between a Project Steering Committee and the Project Manager is analogous to that of a Company Board and the Chief Executive. A Board recruits a Chief Executive and, in partnership with him or her, sets the strategic direction of the company, but the Chief Executive is responsible for the day-to-day running of the company and the results achieved.

Similarly, the Project Manager is responsible for the day-to-day running of the project, the goal and cost of which will have been determined by him or her in partnership with the Steering Committee.

Like a Company Board, a Project Steering Committee should not be too hands-on. The Project Manager runs the project in accordance with the agreed specification.

However, like a Company Board, the Steering Committee should not be too casual, either. Steering Committee members should read the project specification and the Project Manager's regular reports carefully. Steering Committee meetings should be minuted, and Steering Committee members should sign key documents – specifically, the project specification, the risk management plan (if a separate document) and formal project checkpoint documents (e.g. tollgate decisions).

Steering Committee membership

The ideal number of people on a Project Steering Committee, including the Project Manager, is five. Why five? An odd number is desirable, so that decisions can be arrived at by a majority vote (although this should rarely be necessary). A number smaller than five will not allow adequate stakeholder representation. A number larger than five will become unwieldy; the Steering Committee's job is direction and decision making, not debating.

Steering Committee members should, in combination, represent all the project stakeholders and have sufficient authority to authorize the release of contingency funds or to terminate the project without reference to anyone else.

To pursue the accounts payable system example, the Chief Financial Officer, who would be the sponsor of such a project, would chair the Steering Committee. The Chief Information Officer, or his or her nominee, would also be a member of the Steering Committee.

Steering Committee function

The Project Steering Committee's functions are to:

1. Provide management support for the project in terms of resources and competencies;
2. Ensure that the project:
   i.   Accords with the organization's business direction
   ii.   Is commercially and financially viable
   iii. Delivers benefits that justify the resources consumed;
3. Analyse the status and progress of the project.

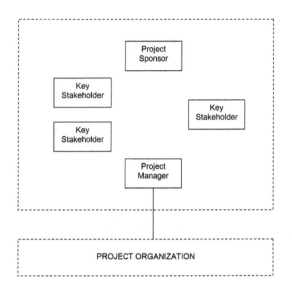

Figure 5: Project Steering Committee

CHAPTER 3: EFFECTIVE PROJECT PLANNING

You want to know how long the project will take, how much it will cost, and who is going to be working on it to the scaling down or exclusion of their normal activities. Project estimates are supposed to supply this information so that you can plan accordingly.

The person compiling the project estimates is making a prediction. Unfortunately, this prediction, almost invariably, becomes a management goal, and a management goal is a potential noose for the person who created it. If the project encounters difficulties, if it exceeds its allotted time and/or its allotted budget, what was called an estimate has become, in many minds, a broken undertaking.

Project Managers are often asked to come up with estimates by a certain date, with no knowledge of or control over project features that are fundamental to the estimating process – including resourcing, equipment, budgetary constraints and application scope. Yet the estimate produced becomes the budget to which the project must conform.

Aware of the purpose of the estimate (i.e. knowing that the estimate will become a management target), a Project Manager will take out insurance. She or he will emphasize at every turn that the figures are based on an assumption that the necessary resources will be made available when required by the project schedule, that the support and co-operation of the end-user community are needed and assumed, that computer upgrades will be made and that necessary software will be installed before the tasks requiring them are scheduled to begin, and so on and so forth.

Projects that begin in this way are almost predestined to fail. If they are completed – and they often aren't – they are highly unlikely to come in on time, and they are highly unlikely to come in on budget.

This happens in organizations that attempt projects without making the structural alterations necessary to accommodate them – organizations lacking the understandings and conditions under which projects may be planned and delivered successfully.

No organization can succeed at projects if every dollar spent on one is begrudged because it puts a hole in the relevant business unit's bottom line.

As I said earlier, it all starts and ends with management accounting.

Accounting for the cost of project planning

Whether a business unit is a cost centre or a profit centre, it needs a line item in its annual budget for project planning.

How might this figure be calculated?

One way could be through discussions between the leader of the business unit and his or her staff to determine how much of their time goes into business and systems analyses, RFPs, feasibility studies and estimating. The business unit leader would then be in a position to calculate the opportunity cost and add it to his or her annual budget (she or he should not subtract it from his or her operational allocation!).

Now the business unit will have funds to plan its projects properly, which means that the organization will be much better positioned to decide whether or not to execute them based on the project specifications produced.

> When the cost of producing project specifications is budgeted for, the quality of those specifications rises dramatically.

Accounting for the time of project planning

I have tried to show that the most difficult thing about projects is that their complexities become apparent only as they unfold.

However thorough the risk assessment, issues will arise during the execution phase to frustrate the project team and exasperate management.

But, as I have also tried to show, the more time allowed for planning prior to the execution phase, the fewer issues there will be and the less severe their effects will be.

There is no rule for how much time should be spent on the planning phase: it must be left to the Project Manager's discretion. She or he will decide, in consultation with the Steering Committee, when no purpose can be served by continuing to defer the decision on whether or not to proceed to the execution phase.

As a rule of thumb, however, you may find the following quadrant useful as a guide to what an organization is letting itself in for when it allows a project to proceed to the execution phase.

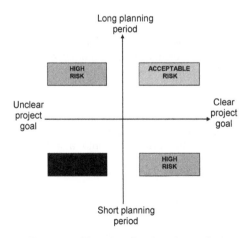

Figure 6: The planning/goal quadrant

Remember, a clear project goal is spelled out in quantifiable terms to the point of pedantry.

To assess whether the planning has been adequate, audit the project specification before presenting it to the Project Steering Committee for approval. Look at the risk management plan. Have the risks been categorized? Have both generic and specific risks been identified? Are the proposed mitigation strategies specific or general? Has responsibility for risk mitigation been assigned to a named individual in each case?

Also, look at how long it is estimated that the project will take to complete. **If the schedule is longer than 12 months, don't approve it.**

Some things, by nature, take longer than 12 months to implement, but if you're not an engineering or construction company, experienced with very large projects, you're asking for trouble. If the proposal is urgent and important, send the project specification back with instructions that it be broken down into two or more dependant (sequential) projects, each taking less than 12 months to complete.

A completed project specification should be examined by your Internal Auditor or Risk Manager before being submitted to the Project Steering Committee for approval.

No single project scheduled to last more than 12 months should be approved. If the goal will take more than a year to attain, break the project up into a set of smaller, sequential projects.

The two types of project

Essentially, any project contemplated by your organization will be one of two distinct types: the strategic positioning project or the efficiency gain project.

I said earlier that the financial return on a project is rarely calculable. This is especially true of strategic positioning projects. These projects are like new ventures – the people providing the capital want to see what they'll get for their investment, but the financial projections are entirely imaginary. No one actually knows how it will work out. So it comes down to how much you're prepared to spend to make it happen.

Efficiency gain projects, on the other hand, are like the new accounts payable system: the intended result is to improve – by speeding up, saving labour, or introducing value-adding features – some existing system or activity. The return on such investments can be calculated to a certain extent. You could, for example, work out the annual cost to the organization – it will usually be an opportunity cost – of doing things the present way. You could then work out the annual cost to the organization of doing things in the better way promised by the new system. How many times do you have to multiply the difference between the two figures before you've reached the estimated cost of the project? Does this represent an acceptable time to wait for the payback?

In both cases, of course, what you're doing is looking at the effect of the project investment on your cash flow. The longer you give your Project Manager to plan the project, the more accurately she or he will be able to predict this – always bearing in mind that **issues will arise during the project and that you should increase the draft budget by 25% to reach an acceptable level of safety.**

Of course, organizations vary widely in terms of the funds they have available for projects and in their willingness to incur risks. All I can say is that my contingency figure of 25% issues from 16 years' experience of managing projects across the public and private and not-for-profit sectors.

You may find the following schematic useful as a complement to the previous planning/goal quadrant.

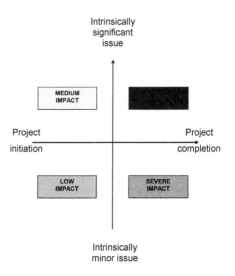

Figure 7: The issue/time quadrant

Once project execution has commenced, the effect of change becomes exponentially more ugly. This is why there should be no built-in disincentive to a thorough planning process.

Project planning is a sunk cost and should be in the annual operating budget of every one of your business units.

A guide to effective project governance

Project governance is the establishment of organizational understandings and conditions under which projects may be planned and delivered successfully.

The following flowchart indicates a few simple steps you can take – once you've incorporated the cost of project planning in your annual operating budgets – to ensure an effective project governance process.

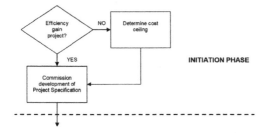

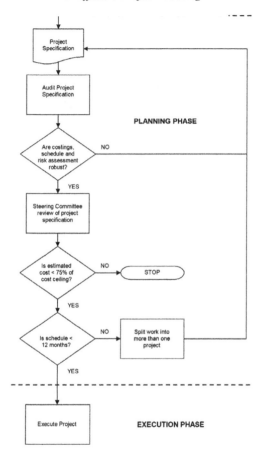

Figure 8:The project planning checkpoints

CHAPTER 4: YOUR ORGANIZATION

What follows is a simple diagnostic. See whether your organization could build the Great Pyramid, or whether it would botch the Sydney Opera House!

1. My organization exists in a complex political environment of numerous committees and influential stakeholders.

Yes: No score

No: One point

You can't help your environment, but if your organization is like this, it will find projects very difficult to plan and deliver successfully. The project planning process will need to be sold to these committees and stakeholders, so that when a project reaches the execution stage it answers to only one committee: the Project Steering Committee.

2. My organization obtains the funds before initiating a major project.

Yes: No score

No: One point

How does your organization know how much the project will cost before the planning phase of the project is complete?

3. My organization is always clear about the desired outcome before giving an assignment to a Project Manager.

Yes: One point

No: No score

A Project Manager can deliver what is required, but a Project Manager is not a mind-reader. The organization needs to know what it wants and why before the Project Manager can work out how long it will take and how much it will cost.

4. My organization would never appoint a Project Manager who wasn't an expert in the relevant business area.

Yes: No score

No: One point

A Project Manager needs to know how to deliver a project, not how to carve the right hieroglyphics in the Pharaoh's burial-chamber. The number of failed projects given to subject matter experts is beyond computation. Good Project Managers know what questions to ask and of whom to ask them. That's how they develop schedules and budgets.

5. My organization includes funds for project planning in the annual budget for each business unit.

Yes: One point

No: No score

No one likes overheads, but the funds involved are a drop in the ocean compared with the cost of project failure.

6. My organization is outcome-focussed. We don't spend hours in meetings – we get on with it.

Yes: No score

No: One point

Being outcome-focussed is good, but a lack of planning is not good. A classic cause of project failure is premature launch (as in the case of the Sydney Opera House). A simple equation shows that every additional day spent on planning at the start of a project saves two weeks of rework at the end of the project. I'm sure you can work out which is cheaper.

7. My organization ensures that business owners are empowered to keep projects in line with their requirements.

Yes: No score

No: One point

If your organization has approved a project, it is by definition in line with business requirements. If people outside the formal governance structure of the project can influence its progress, you are set up for failure.

8. Performance in project work is factored into the annual Key Performance Indicators (KPIs) of all our staff.

Yes: One point

No: No score

IT projects, in particular, work on the matrix principle – operational staff will be involved in the project because of their specific expertise. If their performance is measured exclusively on their operational work, however, there is a built-in disincentive for them – and for their line managers – to lend support to the project.

9. My organization always ensures that project suppliers are bound by legally enforceable contracts.

Yes: No score

No: One point

Mutual recrimination and protracted, expensive court cases are a poor substitute for a successful project. A clear and concise Statement of Work is far more valuable than any number of liquidated damages clauses. It also guarantees, unlike a long and complicated legal contract, that your organization and the supplier agree about what needs to be done and how to do it.

10. My organization has established procedures to ensure that contract staff required for a project are equipped with desks, building access passes, computers and telephones on the day they arrive.

Yes: One point

No: No score

If your organization doesn't have such procedures in place, it is haemorrhaging money. Contractors are expensive enough as it is; the cost of unproductive contractors is positively terrifying!

11. My organization would convene a special meeting of all stakeholders if a project was perceived to be in trouble.

Yes: No score

No: One point

If your project was properly governed, there would be no need for a special meeting – problems would be dealt with as part of the normal course of the project.

12. My organization finishes what it starts. If a project is in trouble, we allocate the additional resources needed to get it back on track.

Yes: No score

No: One point

Throwing resources at a flagging project is a classic sign of failure. Additional resources do not compensate for poor planning (if these resources are needed now, why weren't they needed earlier?). Nor do they compensate for poor governance (why were the problems allowed to become this serious before being addressed?). Besides, will additional resources fix the problems? Can you be sure you aren't throwing good money after bad?

Your organization's score

0 – 4: Ouch! Your organization may be outstandingly successful in operational terms, but it's a basket case when it comes to projects. If you're thinking about a major project, I strongly suggest you get some outside help – *not* to manage the project, but to recommend the changes needed within your organization before it should contemplate *attempting* a project.

5 – 8: Well, it may or may not console you to know that your organization is roughly the same as every other organization when it comes to projects. You win some, you lose some. But I can guarantee that, with a little attention to the governance issues discussed in this book, your organization will be able to deliver projects faster, cheaper and more reliably than in the past.

9 – 12: Congratulations! Your organization is in the top bracket when it comes to maturity of project management practice. Please contact me with suggestions as to how this book might be improved.

CHAPTER 5: DO YOU MEAN IT?

The Project Manager has presented an impressively thorough project specification. It estimates that the project will cost $1.5 million and will take eight months to complete. The estimates have been verified by your Internal Auditor.

Why should you add to this carefully worked out budget?

Because human beings cannot predict the future; because issues will arise as surely as night follows day; and because you want a margin for error, not an undertaking that will almost certainly be broken.

Add 25% to the budget, making it $1.875 million. Determine the relevant cash flows and discount them. If the net present value of the project is still positive, it can proceed to the execution stage.

Doing this is not giving licence to excess or reckless expenditure – it is insuring the project and your organization against the unexpected. If the project comes in at around $1.5 million, excellent – the additional $375 thousand earmarked for project overrun can be reinvested. But if something happens to derange the project budget, additional funds can be obtained without robbing some other area of your organization.

> Whether, and under what circumstances. project contingency funds should be committed is entirely a matter for the Project Steering Committee.

Project governance self-test

What have we learned? See how you respond to the following questions.

1. Project governance is:
   a) A matter for project management specialists
   b) An organizational issue

c) The province of the Project Steering Committee
d) The responsibility of the Project Manager.

2. Project failure is usually attributable to:
   a) Unreliable suppliers
   b) An inexperienced Project Manager
   c) Changing requirements
   d) Inadequate planning.

3. Project cost containment is best achieved by:
   a) Budgeting precisely for every line item
   b) Auditing the project regularly
   c) Thorough planning and built-in contingency
   d) Using the cheapest suppliers and materials.

4. Successful projects are distinguished by:
   a) A simple and direct reporting and communication structure
   b) Their subordination to the operational requirements of the organization
   c) Top management representation on the Project Steering Committee
   d) No changes to the original specifications.

The correct answers are: 1(b), 2(d), 3(c) and 4(a).

Project governance is an organizational issue. Project failure is usually – I would even go so far as to say always – attributable to inadequate planning. Project cost containment is best achieved by thorough planning and built-in contingency (25% of the estimate). Successful projects are distinguished by simple and direct reporting and communication structures, i.e. a Project Steering Committee composed of the Project Manager and four others who, between them, represent the project's key stakeholders.

Now ask yourself the following questions:

---

1. Am I prepared to allocate the time and resources necessary to plan projects in the fashion described in this book?

---

2. Am I prepared to make the necessary adjustments to my organization's accounting procedures to allow effective project governance?

---

3. Am I prepared to devolve full powers upon the Project Steering Committee once the project has been approved to proceed to the execution stage?

---

4. Do I understand why the most important project audit is that undertaken before the project moves to the execution stage?

I hope you can see why I'm hoping that your answer to each of these questions was yes.

Oscar Wilde observed that the truth is rarely pure and never simple. He could have been talking about projects. The logic of management accounting makes direction of funds to planning activities difficult. The devolution of power from senior executives to a temporary committee is counter-intuitive. Auditing something that hasn't begun is, on the face of it, downright bizarre. But these are the keys to project success.

The good news is that these steps are easy to take. You do not have to spend any money you don't already have. You risk nothing by empowering those most closely concerned with the outcome of a project. You waste nothing by expanding the remit of your Internal Auditor.

By taking these simple steps, you will have established a strong project governance framework in your organization, thereby ensuring a dramatic rise in your project success-rate.

Project governance is the establishment of organizational understandings and conditions under which projects may be planned and delivered successfully.

Good luck!

FURTHER READING

The following is a very short list of material you may find useful to supplement what I have written.

- Elton, Jeffrey and Justin Roe. 'Bringing Discipline to Project Management.' *Harvard Business Review,* Vol. 86, No. 2, March-April (1998), pp. 153-59.

  A valuable discussion based on Eli Goldratt's theory of constraints.

- Flyvbjerg, Bent. 'Design by Deception: The Politics of Megaproject Approval.' *Harvard Design Magazine,* No. 22, Spring/Summer (2005), pp. 50-9.

  An exposé of the crippling effects of misgovernment on major projects.

- ISACA®.[1] *COBIT 4.1, PO10 Manage Projects.*

  Obtainable from *www.isaca.org/cobit*

  COBIT® is an IT governance framework and supporting toolset that allows managers to bridge the gap between control requirements, technical issues and business risks.

- ISACA®. *COBIT Mapping: Mapping PMBOK to COBIT 4.0.*

  Obtainable from *www.isaca.org/Knowledge-Center/Research/ResearchDeliverables/Pages/COBIT-Mapping-Mapping-PMBOK-with-COBIT-4-0.aspx*

- Kappelman, Leon A., Robert McKeeman and Lixuan Zhang. 'Early Warning Signs of IT Project Failure: The

---

[1] Formerly the Information Systems Audit and Control Association, ISACA is now known by its initials only, to reflect the broad range of IT governance professionals it serves.

Dominant Dozen.' *Information Systems Management*, Vol. 23, No. 4, Fall (2006), pp. 31-6.

Obtainable from *www.ism-journal.com/ITToday/projectfailure.pdf*

- Needham, Keith. 'Project management auditing theory: Practical experience and examples.' Grant Thornton UK LLP: 2010.

  Contact: *Keith.Needham@uk.gt.com*

- Project Management Institute. *A Guide to the Project Management Body of Knowledge (PMBOK® Guide)*. 4th edn. Newtown Square, PA: Project Management Institute, 2008.

  Obtainable from *www.pmi.org/PMBOK-Guide-and-Standards/Standards-Library-of-PMI-Global-Standards-Projects.aspx*

  The Project Management Institute (PMI) is the world's leading not-for-profit membership association for the project management profession, with more than half a million members and credential holders in 185 countries. The *Project Management Body of Knowledge (PMBOK)* explains the various aspects of project management. It is a set of principles, not a method.

- Schmitt, John W. and Kenneth A. Kozar. 'Management's Role in Information System Development Failures: A Case Study.' *MIS Quarterly*, Vol. 2, No. 2, June (1978), pp. 7-16.

  Do not be put off by the age of this article; the issues it raises are timeless.

- Swanson, Dan. 'Auditing IT Initiatives Is a Recommended Quality Practice.' *New Perspectives*, Association of Healthcare Internal Auditors, August (2008), pp. 23-5.

  Obtainable from

www.ahia.org/audit_library/newperspectivesarchive/new_perspectives/2008/Summer2008/TheITPerspectiveColumn_AuditingITInitiativesIsaRecommendedQualityPracticebyDanSwanson.pdf

- The Information Technology Advisory Committee (ITAC). *20 Questions Directors Should Ask about IT Projects.* Toronto: The Canadian Institute of Chartered Accountants, 2007.

  Obtainable from
  http://www.cica.ca/ifrs/ifrs-transition-resources/docs-&-files/item2411.pdf

- Wegrzynowicz, Karine and Steve Stein. *Auditing IT Projects.* Global Technology Audit Guide (GTAG®) 12. Altamonte Springs, FL: The Institute of Internal Auditors, 2009.

  Obtainable from

  www.theiia.org/guidance/technology/gtag12/

ITG RESOURCES

IT Governance Ltd. sources, creates and delivers products and services to meet the real-world, evolving IT governance needs of today's organisations, directors, managers and practitioners. The ITG website (*www.itgovernance.co.uk*) is the international one-stop-shop for corporate and IT governance information, advice, guidance, books, tools, training and consultancy.

http://www.itgovernance.co.uk/project_governance.aspx is the information page on our website for our project governance resources.

Other Websites

Books and tools published by IT Governance Publishing (ITGP) are available from all business booksellers and are also immediately available from the following websites:

www.itgovernance.co.uk/catalog/355 provides information and online purchasing facilities for every currently available book published by ITGP.

www.itgovernance.eu is our euro-denominated website which ships from Benelux and has a growing range of books in European languages other than English.

www.itgovernanceusa.com is a US$-based website that delivers the full range of IT Governance products to North America, and ships from within the continental US.

www.itgovernanceasia.com provides a selected range of ITGP products specifically for customers in South Asia.

www.27001.com is the IT Governance Ltd. website that deals specifically with information security management, and ships from within the continental US.

Pocket Guides

For full details of the entire range of pocket guides, simply follow the links at *www.itgovernance.co.uk/publishing.aspx*.

Toolkits

ITG's unique range of toolkits includes the IT Governance Framework Toolkit, which contains all the tools and guidance that you will need in order to develop and implement an appropriate IT governance framework for your organisation. Full details can be found at *www.itgovernance.co.uk/ products/519*.

For a free paper on how to use the proprietary Calder-Moir IT Governance Framework, and for a free trial version of the toolkit, see *www.itgovernance.co.uk/calder_moir.aspx*.

There is also a wide range of toolkits to simplify implementation of management systems, such as an ISO/IEC 27001 ISMS or a BS25999 BCMS, and these can all be viewed and purchased online at: *http://www.itgovernance.co.uk/catalog/1*.

Best Practice Reports

ITG's range of Best Practice Reports is now at *www.itgovernance.co.uk/best-practice-reports.aspx*. These offer you essential, pertinent, expertly researched information on a number of key issues including Web 2.0 and Green IT.

Training and Consultancy

IT Governance also offers training and consultancy services across the entire spectrum of disciplines in the information governance arena. Details of training courses can be accessed at *www.itgovernance.co.uk/training.aspx* and descriptions of our consultancy services can be found at *http://www.itgovernance.co.uk/consulting.aspx*.
Why not contact us to see how we could help you and your organisation?

Newsletter

IT governance is one of the hottest topics in business today, not least because it is also the fastest moving, so what better way to keep up than by subscribing to ITG's free monthly newsletter *Sentinel*? It provides monthly updates and resources across the whole spectrum of IT governance subject matter, including risk management, information security, ITIL and IT service management, project governance, compliance and so much more. Subscribe   for   your   free   copy   at: *www.itgovernance.co.uk/newsletter.aspx*.

Lightning Source UK Ltd.
Milton Keynes UK
UKOW06f0839200416

272615UK00016B/244/P